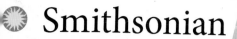

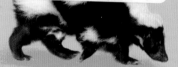

STINKY, STICKY, SNEAKY STUFF

BY **TRACEY WEST**

Grosset & Dunlap
An Imprint of Penguin Random House

GROSSET & DUNLAP

Penguin Young Readers Group
An Imprint of Penguin Random House LLC

✳ Smithsonian

This trademark is owned by the Smithsonian Institution and
is registered in the U.S. Patent and Trademark Office.

Smithsonian Enterprises:
Christopher Liedel, President
Carol LeBlanc, Senior Vice President, Education and Consumer Products
Brigid Ferraro, Vice President, Education and Consumer Products
Ellen Nanney, Licensing Manager
Kealy Gordon, Product Development Manager

Smithsonian Institution, National Museum of Natural History:
Dr. Don E. Wilson, Curator Emeritus, Department of Vertebrate Zoology

Library of Congress Cataloging-in-Publication Data is available.

ISBN 9780448486901   10 9 8 7 6 5 4 3 2 1

CONTENTS

ALL ABOUT STUFF THAT IS ...
STINKY, STICKY,
or SNEAKY!

Ever wonder why feet can be stinky?
Or why glue is sticky?
Or what spies use to be sneaky?

Then this book is for you!
Inside you'll read all about stuff that will
make you say, "NO WAY!" ... but "WAY!"
Everything in this book is 100% true!

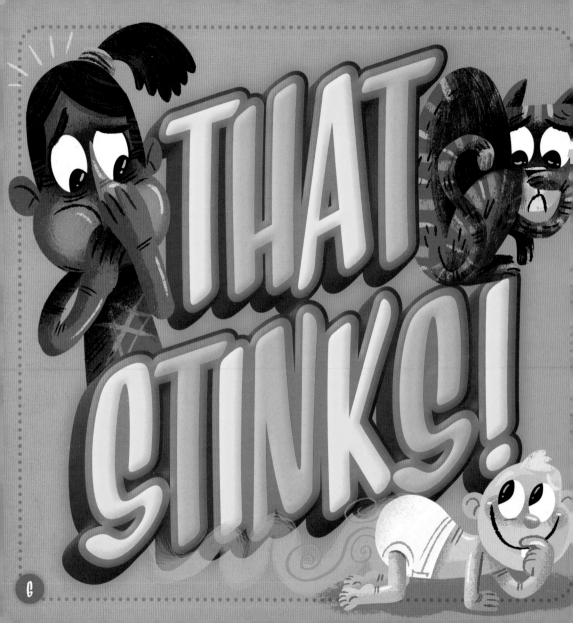

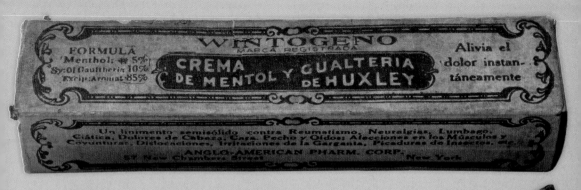

Smell and smell alike? No way! According to a 1966 study, Americans thought wintergreen smelled great. British people thought it stunk like medicine.

Nares is another word for nostrils.

Humans can detect one trillion different scents.

No Way!

NOT STINKY!

Vanilla, cinnamon, and crayons are among the scents that people like best.

9

YOU CAN SMELL FEELINGS OF FEAR AND DISGUST THROUGH SWEAT.

A DNA test can't tell identical twins apart—but a trained dog can smell the difference.

THE AFRICAN ELEPHANT IS THE TOP SNIFFER, WITH 1,948 GENES DEDICATED TO SCENT. (HUMANS HAVE 396.)

LE
Restaurant Stinké

APPETIZERS

VIEUX BOULOGNE CHEESE

WAS NAMED THE STINKIEST CHEESE IN A STUDY JUDGED BY HUMANS AND AN ELECTRONIC NOSE.

· ·

SURSTRÖMMING

THE SWEDISH GOVERNMENT WARNS THAT YOU SHOULD OPEN THE TIN OF THIS FERMENTED HERRING OUTSIDE. IT IS SAID TO SMELL LIKE GARBAGE LEFT IN THE SUN.

NATTO

THESE FERMENTED SOYBEANS GIVE
OFF THE ODOR OF SMELLY SOCKS.

• •

KOREAN DOENJANG

IS A PASTE MADE OF DRIED SOYBEANS
THAT SMELLS LIKE AMMONIA. WHY? BACTERIA
GIVE OFF THE ODOR DURING FERMENTATION.

MAIN COURSE

STINKY TOFU

IS A POPULAR DISH IN TAIWAN! IT MAY SMELL
LIKE AN OPEN SEWER OR DIRTY FEET, BUT
PEOPLE SAY YOU CAN'T TASTE THE STINKINESS.

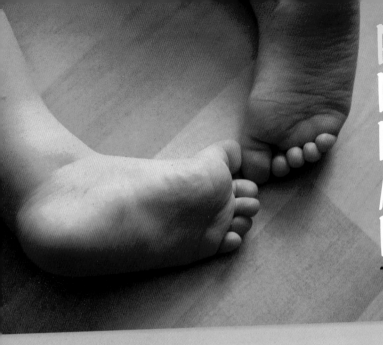

BACTERIA LOVE DARK, SWEATY PLACES, LIKE ARMPITS AND BETWEEN YOUR TOES.

SCIENTISTS HAVE FOUND THAT WHEN BACTERIA BREAK DOWN SWEAT, THIOALCOHOLS THAT CAN SMELL LIKE "SULFUR, ONIONS OR MEAT" ARE PRODUCED.

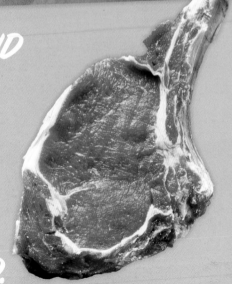

Antiperspirants work by blocking sweat glands and/or killing bacteria.

IN 1948, A **HIKER** WORE THESE **BOOTS** ALONG THE ENTIRE APPALACHIAN TRAIL, WHICH RUNS 2,180 MILES (3,508 KM), FROM GEORGIA TO MAINE. THE BOOTS ARE NOW IN THE SMITHSONIAN'S COLLECTION— AND THEY STILL **STINK!**

BACTERIA EAT THE **DEAD SKIN CELLS** IN YOUR FEET AND THEN GET RID OF WASTE IN ORGANIC ACIDS. THAT'S WHAT SMELLS BAD.

Really stinky feet are caused by sweat-loving bacteria that produce volatile sulfur compounds (the same smell as rotten eggs).

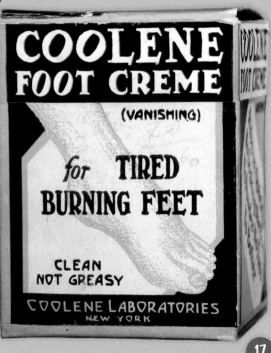

17

BAD-BREATH BUDDIES:

A PALEO DIET (WHAT EARLY HUMANS ATE): SMELLY KETONES ARE RELEASED IN YOUR BREATH AS YOUR BODY BURNS FAT.

SLEEPING: YOUR SALIVA DRIES OUT WHEN YOU SLEEP, AND BACTERIA THRIVE.

ALLERGIES: BAD-BREATH-CAUSING BACTERIA LOVE TO DINE ON THE MUCUS IN YOUR THROAT.

CAVITIES!

KEEP YOUR

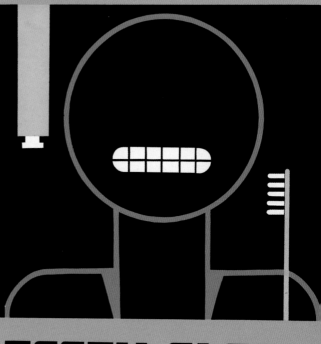

TEETH CLEAN

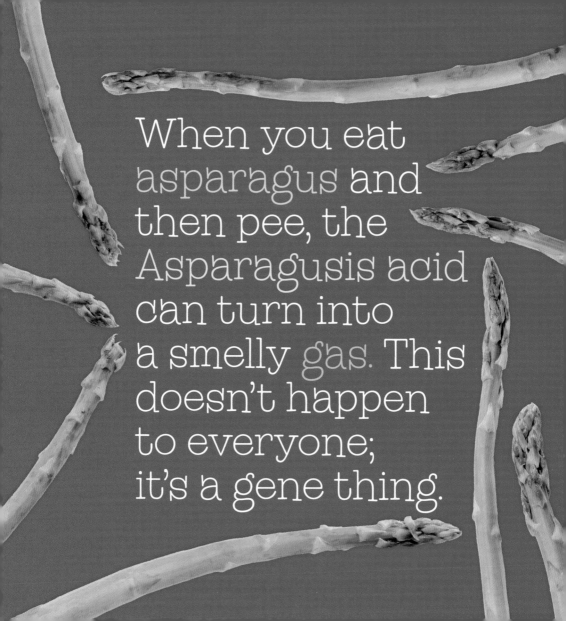

When you eat asparagus and then pee, the Asparagusis acid can turn into a smelly gas. This doesn't happen to everyone; it's a gene thing.

THE AVERAGE PERSON PASSES GAS TEN TIMES A DAY.

If you fart on a plane, the seat absorbs half the odor (but only half!).

When you eat garlic, onions, and curry, the smell will come through the pores of your skin when you sweat.

EATING GARLIC MIGHT KEEP AWAY INSECTS!

BEFORE HOMES HAD TOILETS, PEOPLE USED CHAMBER POTS, HOLES IN THE GROUND, AND OUTHOUSES.

24

SOME OUTHOUSE DOORS HAVE A CRESCENT MOON CUT OUT TO LET IN LIGHT AND AIR.

EVERY YEAR IN MICHIGAN, PEOPLE RACE OUTHOUSES ON SKIS.

garderobe

QUEEN ELIZABETH I'S GODSON INVENTED THE FLUSHING TOILET IN 1596.

Queen Elizabeth I

MIDDLE AGES: IF YOU HAD TO POOP IN A MEDIEVAL ENGLISH CASTLE, YOU ENTERED THE GARDEROBE, A CLOSET WITH A **HOLE** IN THE FLOOR. WASTE DROPPED INTO THE **MOAT** BELOW.

THE BRITISH MONARCH HAD ONE IN HER PALACE, BUT IT TOOK ALMOST 200 YEARS FOR THE TREND TO CATCH ON!

IN 1775, ALEXANDER CUMMINGS INVENTED AN S-SHAPED PIPE TO KEEP OUT FOUL ODORS CAUSED BY INDOOR PLUMBING. WAY!

The first garbage men were probably English "rakers" who cleaned up the garbage in the streets during the "black plague" of the 1300s.

The first garbage trucks were horse-drawn carts.

The Garwood Load Packer (1938) was the first garbage truck to use hydraulic blades to push the trash into the back of the truck.

When dogs roll in stinky stuff, they might be masking their scent before a hunt, just like their wolf ancestors.

When a dog smells urine it can tell if the animal is male or female, how healthy it is, and even what mood it's in.

A DOG COULD SNIFF OUT A TEASPOON OF SUGAR IN A MILLION GALLONS OF WATER.

ANIMAL ODORS and PLANT P-Us

A plant that smells like a skunk? NO WAY!

WAY!

Meet the bog-dwelling skunk cabbage.

A skunk can hit a target up to 12 feet away with its spray.

A spotted skunk will perform a handstand when it sprays.

When a skunk sprays, you can smell the odor over one mile away.

SOME PEOPLE ARE ALLERGIC TO THE SMELL OF **COCKROACHES** AND **STINK BUGS.**

SCIENTISTS TRACKED ONE STINK BUG THAT FLEW 75 MILES IN A SINGLE DAY.

STINK BUGS ARE HARD TO GET RID OF BECAUSE THEY HAVE NO NATURAL PREDATORS.

The South American hoatzin is called the "stink bird."

It has a digestive system like a cow: The hoatzin ferments food in its stomach and produces stinky manure.

The African green wood hoopoe squirts stinky liquid poo when attacked.

Sea birds called fulmars vomit up smelly stomach oils to ward off attackers.

The Blackfoot people call the wolverine the "skunk bear."

Wolverines' stinky scent comes from their strong musk glands.

The musk ox also has strong musk glands. (Duh!)

These hairy oxen release musk in their urine, and it gets stuck in their fur. (Yuck!)

The honey badger has a stink gland like a skunk, but it drops a "stink bomb" instead of spraying.

Ring-tailed lemurs compete for mates in a "stink-off."

They repel each other using the smelly glands on their wrists and shoulders.

YOU CAN SMELL THE STINK OF A TAMANDUA FROM MORE THAN 160 FEET AWAY!

JAGUARS DON'T LIKE THE STINK OF TAMANDUAS, SO THEY STAY AWAY.

THE TASMANIAN DEVIL IS ONLY STINKY WHEN IT'S STRESSED.

The **corpse flower** emits the odor of rotting meat to attract carrion flies.

A **corpse flower** is about 3 feet wide. That's one big stinking flower!

STICK AROUND!

Caulobacter crescentus is a bacteria that makes a sugary substance so super sticky, one drop could hold up a pickup truck. **49**

EARLY CAVE PAINTERS MIXED PAINT
WITH GLUE SO IT WOULD LAST. (IT DID!)

More than 3,000 years ago, Egyptians glued their furniture together.

What do fish bones, animal hides, vegetables, and petroleum have in common? They are all used to make glue!

51

Zinc oxide, the stuff in sunscreen, is what makes school glue white.

STRONGEST GLUE:
IN 2012, SCOTCH WELD
LIFTED AN 8.1-TON
FORKLIFT INTO THE
AIR FOR ONE HOUR!

53

NO WAY! A SNEEZE CAN SHOOT STICKY SNOT OUT AT 60 MILES PER HOUR, UP TO 30 FEET. WAY!

AN EARLY THOMAS EDISON MOVIE SHOWED A MAN SNEEZING.

Snot + air = dried-out snot, otherwise known as a booger.

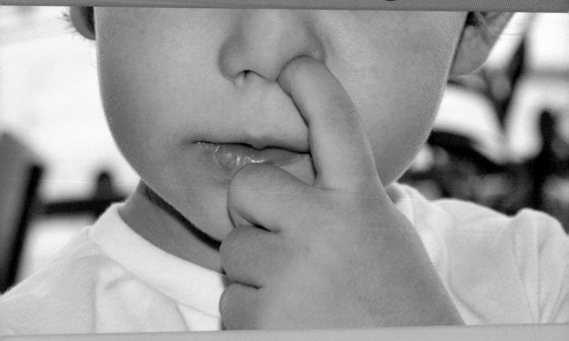

YOUR NOSE MAKES 1 LITER (ALMOST 34 OUNCES) OF STICKY MUCUS A DAY.

A CHOIR SINGER WANTED A BOOKMARK THAT WOULD STICK TO HIS HYMNAL PAGES—SO HE HELPED INVENT THE POST-IT NOTE!

THE FIRST STICKY NOTES ONLY CAME IN YELLOW.

Some people make art out of sticky notes.

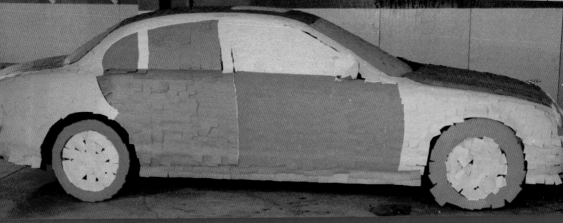

IT TAKES ABOUT 2,000 STICKY NOTES TO COVER A SMALL CAR.

STICKY INVENTOR: RICHARD DREW INVENTED BOTH MASKING TAPE AND CLEAR CELLOPHANE TAPE.

CLEAR ADHESIVE TAPE WAS INVENTED DURING THE GREAT DEPRESSION TO HELP PEOPLE MAKE SIMPLE REPAIRS TO HOUSEHOLD ITEMS.

AN AVERAGE ROLL OF MASKING TAPE IS 60 YARDS LONG—OR ABOUT THE SAME AS THE HEIGHT OF THE LEANING TOWER OF PISA IN ITALY.

Duct tape was invented during World War II to repair military vehicles.

The first duct tape was army green. It became gray when people started using it to fix ducts.

NASA space missions carry duct tape for emergencies.

IT'S 1880. THERE ARE LOTS OF HORSES, LOTS OF MANURE, AND LOTS OF FLIES. WHAT DO YOU DO? INVENT STICKY FLYPAPER!

DRUGGISTS PAINTED THE STICKY STUFF ON PAPER FOR YOU AT THEIR STORES.

TANGLEFOOT SOLD ONE OF THE FIRST FLYPAPERS THAT ALREADY CAME WITH ADHESIVE.

Christmas 10c U.S.

Currier and Ives

Peace on Earth

Christmas

PRECANCELED

U.S. 10 c

You once had to lick stamps to use them. They were coated with cornstarch and dextrin on one side. Yummy? No way!

The first no-lick postage stamps failed in 1974 because the glue didn't work.

Champion licker: Deepak Sharma Bajagain of Nepal licked 70 stamps in one minute in 2010.

Sticky ABC (already-been-chewed) gum is the second most common form of litter after cigarette butts.

Swiss engineer George de Mestral invented Velcro® in the late 1940s.

He was inspired by little hooks on plant burrs that attached themselves to his pants.

NASA astronauts use Velcro® to keep dinner plates from floating away in space, to keep a drink pouch handy, to anchor chess pieces, or to play darts.

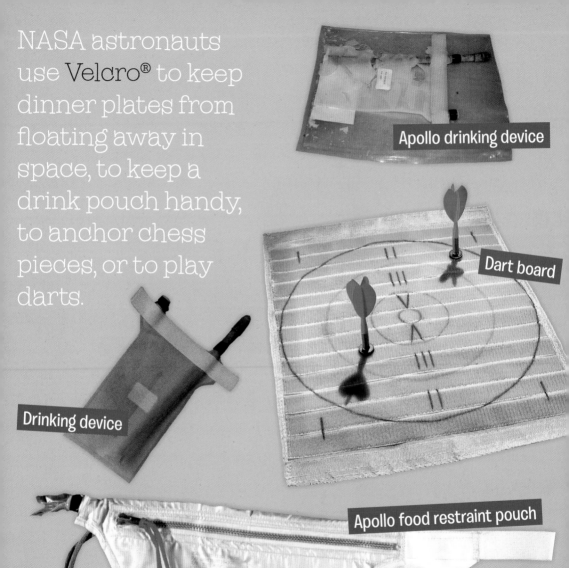

Apollo drinking device

Dart board

Drinking device

Apollo food restraint pouch

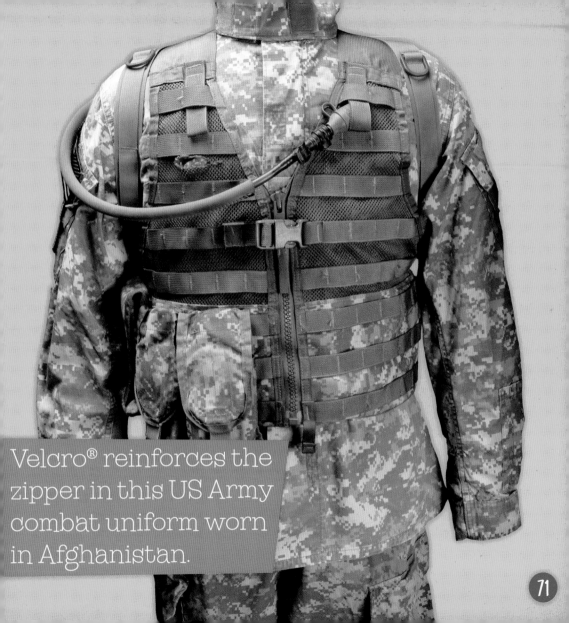

Velcro® reinforces the zipper in this US Army combat uniform worn in Afghanistan.

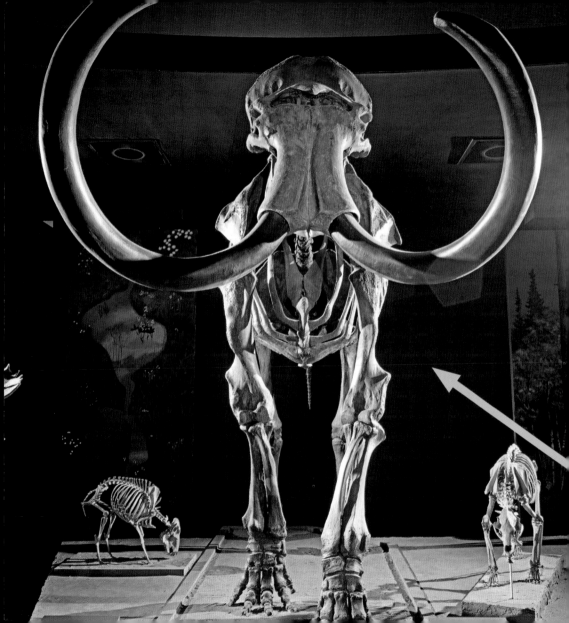

More than 1 million bones have been recovered from the La Brea Tar Pits in Los Angeles.

Animals got trapped in the warm, sticky **asphalt** thousands of years ago.

Scientists discovered the skeleton of a mammoth in the tar pits in 2009—and named him Zed.

WHICH MAMMAL GOT STUCK THE MOST?

THE DIRE WOLF.

FARE! Kviksand
DANGER! Quicksand
ACHTUNG! Quicksand

QUICKSAND CAN BE FOUND ANYWHERE SAND AND WATER MEET.

IF YOU STEP INTO QUICKSAND, WILL YOU SINK BELOW YOUR HEAD AND DROWN? **NO WAY!** THAT'S A MYTH. BUT YOU WILL GET STUCK!

IF YOU DO GET STUCK, SLOWLY WRIGGLE YOUR LEGS AROUND TO LOOSEN THE QUICKSAND.

THERE IS NO QUICKSAND IN QUICKSAND, KENTUCKY (AS FAR AS ANYBODY KNOWS).

Leaf hairs on the sundew plant look like drops of sweet nectar but act like glue to trap insects.

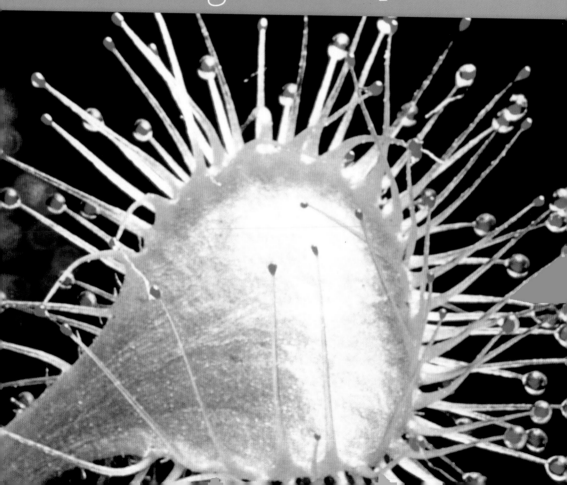

The hooked hairs on the galium aparine plant are so sticky that the plant is called "sticky willy."

The sticky stem of the catchfly plant stops ants from crawling up into its flower.

Trees produce sticky resin to repair wounds to their bark.

Millions of years ago, plants and insects got stuck in tree resin. The resin fossilized into amber, preserving the specimens.

STICKY ANIMALS!

Flies have sticky, hairy feet that help them walk on ceilings.

Each foot has a pair of claws to get the fly unstuck with each step.

81

The horned frog's tongue is so sticky that it can capture lizards, mice, and other frogs.

The tongue has a pulling force of at least 3 times the frog's body weight.

If you had the horned frog's tongue, you could latch on to a baby elephant and pull it toward you!

A spider's stomach produces a glue that it uses to make its web strands sticky.

Sticky spider glue can stretch and stretch, so the spider's victim can't get away before the spider eats it.

Spiderweb strands are stronger and tougher than steel.

Spiderwebs need moisture to stay sticky.

85

Scientists think that spiders spin both sticky and non-sticky threads.

They walk on the non-sticky threads so they don't get stuck.

An orb weaver spider may eat its old web and spin a new one every night.

The Darwin's bark spider can weave a web wide enough to span a river 82 feet across.

A gecko can travel upside down across a smooth ceiling.

A gecko can stick and unstick its feet instantly.

It has millions of tiny hairs on the bottom of its feet called setae.

These hairs stick to surfaces as the gecko slides along.

Engineers are studying gecko feet to make wall-climbing robots.

89

Giraffes are vegetarians.

Their 20-inch-long tongues help them reach leaves.

A giraffe's tongue has extra-thick saliva to protect it from the thorns of the acacia tree, a favorite food.

The dark blue-black color of a giraffe's tongue might act as sunscreen, or it might scare away predators.

A slug's slime helps it climb vertical surfaces.

Slime acts as sunscreen for snails and slugs.

Why is it so hard to wash slug slime off your hands? The sticky stuff absorbs water!

Doctors hope the sticky mucus from the giant African land snail can be used to mend broken bones.

MUSSELS STICK TO ROCKS WITH THIN, STICKY THREADS THAT ARE STRONG ENOUGH TO WITHSTAND CRASHING WAVES.

THE CHRYSALIS OF A GLASSWING BUTTERFLY HOOKS TO THE UNDERSIDE OF A LEAF.

THE HOOKS CAN HOLD FAST EVEN THROUGH HURRICANES.

95

A giant anteater's two-foot-long tongue can scoop up about 30,000 ants a day.

What makes the tongue sticky? Lots of saliva!

Anteaters have no teeth. They swallow their food whole.

Sugar and gelatin combine to make gummy candies sticky.

Gummy bears were around about 60 years before gummy worms.

Good for business: A dentist was one of the first inventors of cotton candy.

UNTIL 1920, *COTTON CANDY* WAS CALLED "FAIRY FLOSS."

COTTON CANDY

Two thousand years ago, pharaohs ate marshmallow candy made from the sticky sap of the mallow plant.

They were the only Egyptians allowed to have the delicious treat.

Today, marshmallows are made with gelatin, not sap.

MAPLE SYRUP IS THE ONLY FOOD CURRENTLY DERIVED FROM PLANT SAP.

MAPLE SYRUP CAN'T FREEZE.

YOU NEED 40 GALLONS OF TREE SAP TO MAKE ONE GALLON OF STICKY MAPLE SYRUP? NO WAY!

WAY! IT ALSO TAKES 5½ DAYS TO COLLECT!

Taffy gets pulled into six-feet-long strands before it's cut into tiny pieces.

Modern machines can produce 1,000 pieces of taffy a minute.

In the days before TV, people had "taffy-pulling" parties for fun.

Saltwater taffy does not contain saltwater.

SALT WATER TAFFY

1,500: the number of PB&J sandwiches the average kid will eat before graduating high school.

Americans on the East Coast prefer creamy peanut butter; on the West Coast they like chunky better.

The first chewing gum was made from **tree** resin.

Bubble gum started out pink because the original inventor had more pink available than any other coloring. It stuck!

GEORGE HERMAN (BABE) RUTH

BIG LEAGUE CHEWING GUM

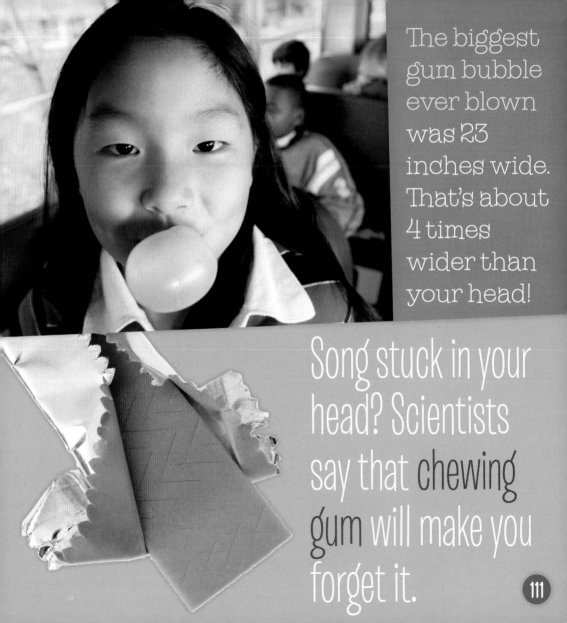

The biggest gum bubble ever blown was 23 inches wide. That's about 4 times wider than your head!

Song stuck in your head? Scientists say that chewing gum will make you forget it.

111

Ancient Egyptians used honey to embalm the dead.

Honey changes flavor and color depending on the nectar used to make it.

Bees must visit 2 million flowers to make one pound of honey.

One ounce of honey is all the fuel a honeybee would need to fly around the world.

STICKY ON A STICK: LOLLIPOPS HAVE PROBABLY BEEN AROUND SINCE THE 1800S.

During the Civil War, some kids may have sucked on hard candies on the ends of their pencils.

Early 1900s: Machines churn out 40 lollipops per minute.
Today: Machines churn out 5,900 lollipops per minute.

I SPY SOMETHING SNEAKY

When the US Civil War began, the man repairing Abraham Lincoln's pocket watch inscribed a secret message inside to show his support for the Union.

117

THE ART OF SECRET WRITING IS CALLED STEGANOGRAPHY.

EARLY RECIPE FOR INVISIBLE INK:

1 Use milk or lemon juice to write between the lines of a letter.

2 Add heat to reveal the writing.

German spies in World War I soaked socks in invisible ink to hide it while traveling. Then they squeezed out the ink to write secret messages.

Ancient Greeks wrote secret messages on tablets, and then covered the tablets in wax.

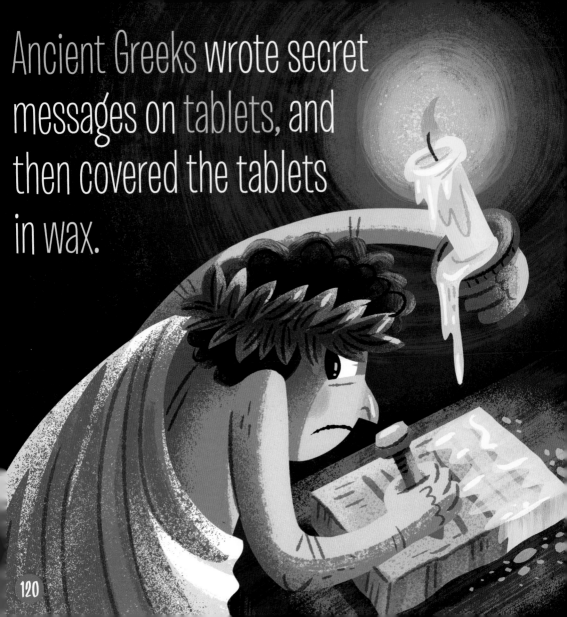

OLD SPY TRICK #1: MAIL AN INNOCENT LETTER TO YOUR FRIEND. WRITE THE REAL MESSAGE UNDERNEATH THE POSTAGE STAMP!

10¢ AIR MAIL

UNITED STATES

FIRST MAN ON THE MOON

OLD SPY TRICK #2: WRITE YOUR MESSAGE IN TINY LETTERS ON A THIN PIECE OF PAPER. ROLL IT UP AND HIDE IT IN AN EMPTY VITAMIN CAPSULE.

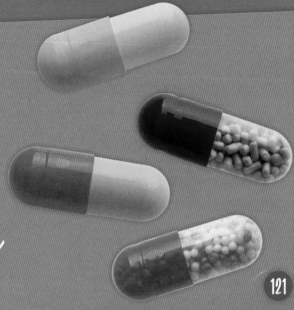

Code = any word or symbol used to represent something else

122

Cipher = a secret message made by changing or rearranging the letters in the words

Simple cipher: Rearrange the letters in a word. On yaw? Awy!

Substitution cipher: Substitute each letter for a different letter or symbol.

Leon Battista Alberti created the first cipher wheel in 1467 to make substitution ciphers easy.

During the American Revolution, Thomas Jefferson and some of the other Founding Fathers communicated through secret ciphers.

Jefferson later invented a cipher wheel made of 36 wooden wheels on an iron rod. His design is still used today.

The Germans invented a series of mechanical cipher devices known as Enigma machines, which they used during World War II.

Two British mathematicians, Alan Turing and Gordon Welchman, designed a machine called **Bombe** that could break any codes created by an Enigma.

In 1844, Samuel Morse invented a code that substituted electrical signals for letters of the alphabet, numbers, and punctuation.

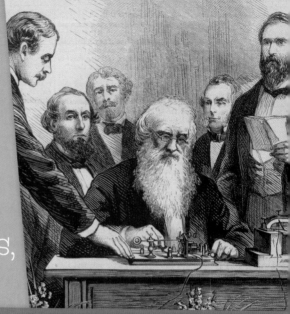

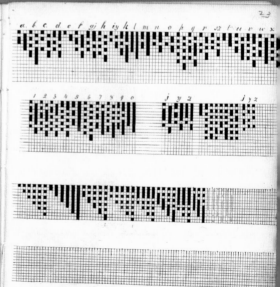

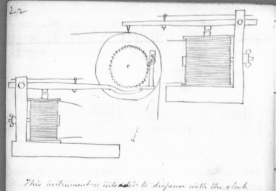

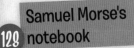

Samuel Morse's notebook

In International Morse Code, each letter is represented by short taps (dots) and long taps (dashes). — • — — — —

• — — • • — • — • — — ?

• — — • • — • — • — — !

The first Morse code telegraph message was, "What hath God wrought?" (This was the first text message!)

The first telegraph receivers typed out the code marks on pieces of paper. That was soon upgraded to beeping sounds.

MORSE CODE

A	• —	N	— •
B	— • • •	O	— — —
C	— • — •	P	• — — •
D	— • •	Q	— — • —
E	•	R	• — •
F	• • — •	S	• • •
G	— — •	T	—
H	• • • •	U	• • —
I	• •	V	• • • —
J	• — — —	W	• — —
K	— • —	X	— • • —
L	• — • •	Y	— • — —
M	— —	Z	— — • •

A "bug" is a listening device that can be hidden in a room or on a person.

A radio transmitter smaller than a postage stamp can be used to relay a conversation to someone with a receiver.

Even easier: Point a laser beam at your target, and the conversation will bounce back to your receiver.

PLAN ATTACK

131

Decoy = sneaky way for hunters to lure animals close to them

JUST ANOTHER DEER HERE: AN APACHE WARRIOR WORE THIS WHILE DEER HUNTING.

SPEAR FISHERMEN USED *FISH DECOYS* LIKE THESE IN THE 1930S.

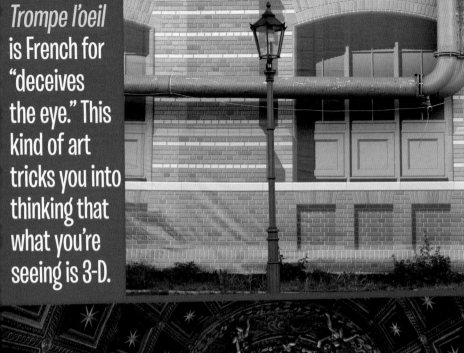

Trompe l'oeil is French for "deceives the eye." This kind of art tricks you into thinking that what you're seeing is 3-D.

The dome of the cathedral in Siena, Italy, appears to open up to the sky—but no way!

ANCIENT GREEK ARTIST ZEUXIS IS SAID TO HAVE PAINTED **GRAPES** SO REAL THAT A **BIRD** TRIED TO EAT THEM.

In the Roman Colosseum, trapdoors opened up, and wolves or boars sprang out to attack unsuspecting gladiators.

Star trap: a trapdoor in a stage. An actor would be lifted up from below, surprising the audience.

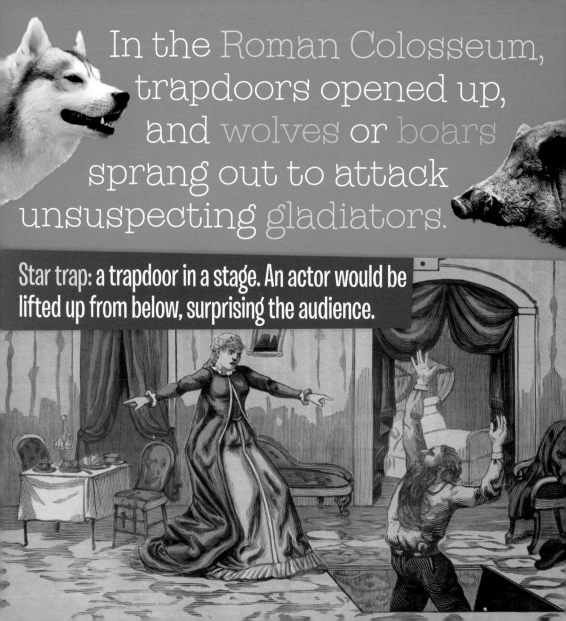

Grave trap: a large, rectangular opening in the middle of a stage floor used for graveyard scenes.

Sneaky: In 1990, two thieves, dressed as Boston police officers, walked into the Isabella Stewart Gardner Museum and stole 13 works of art worth $500 million.

They were never caught.

Not Sneaky: In 1963, the "Great Train Robbers" stole millions from a train in England without a single gun. They played a game of Monopoly with the stolen cash, leaving fingerprints that led to their capture.

Not Sneaky: In 2000, thieves blasted into the Millennium Dome, stealing hundreds of millions of dollars in diamonds. They got caught escaping.

Sneaky: In 2010, robbers used tools to burrow underground into Paris bank vaults and robbed 100 safety deposit boxes. They've never been caught.

Sneaky?: In 1971, a man known as "D.B. Cooper" hijacked a plane, demanded $200,000, and then escaped via parachute. He got away with it—if he survived the jump.

WAR IS... SNEAKY!

Major Benjamin Tallmadge, General George Washington's chief intelligence officer, organized a spy ring against the British during the American Revolution. Tallmadge led the second regiment of the Continental Light Dragoons, whose motto was, "The country expects its sons to respond with tones of thunder."

Patience Lovell Wright, a famous wax sculptor, supported the colonists during the Revolutionary War.

She spied on the British while she was in London and sent letters to America hidden in wax busts.

American general Benedict Arnold gave up secrets to the British during the Revolution, becoming a famous traitor.

Arnold's British contact, Major John André, was captured and hanged. Arnold escaped.

Real Housewife of the Civil War: Socialite Rose O'Neal Greenhow spied for the Confederacy.

She died during a spy mission when her boat sank, weighed down by gold coins.

148

Teen Spy of the Civil War: When Union soldiers came to 19-year-old Belle Boyd's southern town, she hung out with them, picked up information, and smuggled it to the Confederacy.

Famous TV chef Julia Child worked for the Office of Strategic Services during World War II, handling top-secret documents.

Roald Dahl, author of *Charlie and the Chocolate Factory*, was part of a British spy ring that spied on the United States to try and get them to join the World War II effort.

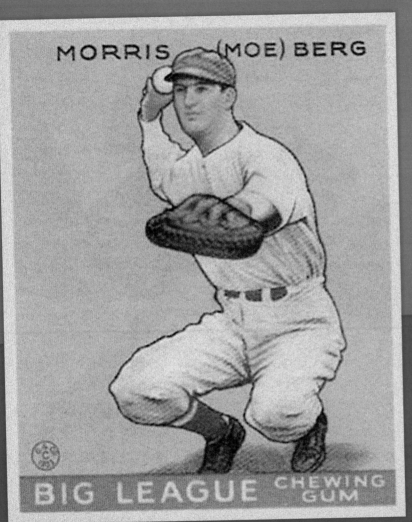

MORRIS (MOE) BERG

BIG LEAGUE CHEWING GUM

Morris "Moe" Berg was a popular Major League Baseball player who became a spy for the Office of Strategic Services in World War II.

Berg spoke seven languages, including Japanese, German, and Russian.

Legendary jazz singer Josephine Baker spied for the French Resistance during World War II.

Since 1960, the US Navy has trained **dolphins** and other marine animals to be spies.

Dolphins can locate underwater mines and drop weights to mark them.

Dolphins can be trained to patrol ports and detect enemy swimmers.

Sea lions can dive as deep as 650 feet underwater to retrieve lost items.

U.S. NAVY

426

The **CIA** trained animal spies during the **Cold War** between the United States and the Soviet Union (c. 1947–1991).

They attached listening devices to cats, turning them into furry transmitters.

Ravens were trained to open file drawers and steal the contents.

In 1944, the FBI arrested two German spies who landed a submarine—in Maine!

Today's FBI employs more than 35,000 people.

Its headquarters are in Washington, DC.

J. Edgar Hoover, the chief of the FBI for 48 years, spied on American politicians and activists.

CENTRAL INTELLIGENCE AGENCY

UNITED STATES OF AMERICA

The 16-point compass on the CIA's shield represents the agency's search for intelligence all over the world.

CIA-trained dogs can sniff out 19,000 explosive scents.

The CIA has a K-9 Hall of Fame.

The CIA has pigeon "agents" that take aerial photos.

The School of Aerial Photography opened in 1918 in Virginia.

In 1956, the US Air Force attached 500 spy cameras to 500 balloons and flew them over the Soviet Union.

The US tried to pass it off as a "meteorological experiment." Many of the cameras were shot down.

Aerial photography allows soldiers to photograph places that were difficult to reach or behind enemy lines.

The US Army Signal Corps manages military communications.

The Signal Corps was established during the Civil War (1861-1865).

The first signalmen communicated using wigwag, a system of sending messages by waving red-and-white flags during the day, and torches at night.

The Signal Corps used carrier pigeons during World War I to deliver messages from the battlefield back to military command.

Radar technology got its start with the Signal Corps in the 1930s.

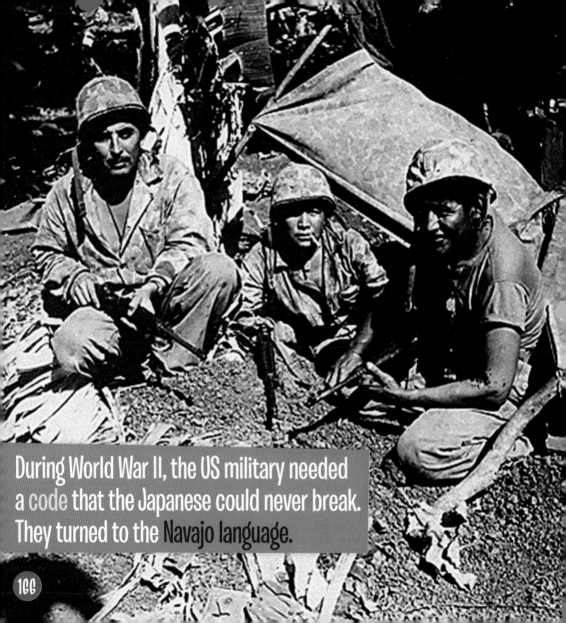

During World War II, the US military needed a code that the Japanese could never break. They turned to the Navajo language.

Navajo "code talkers" participated in every assault the US Marines conducted in the Pacific between 1942 and 1945.

Code talkers could translate a message into Navajo and transmit it in 20 seconds—that's 90 times faster than the regular code machine!

The Japanese never broke the code!

The Navajo language did not have words for modern military terms. So the code talkers invented them:

Besh-be-cha-he
IRON HAT = GERMANY

Besh-lo
IRON FISH = SUBMARINE

Besh-legai-nah-kih
TWO SILVER BARS = CAPTAIN

Ca-lo
SHARK = DESTROYER

Dah-he-tih-hi
HUMMINGBIRD = FIGHTER PLANE

Ga-gih
CROW = PATROL PLANE

Gini
CHICKEN HAWK = DIVE-BOMBER

Hash-kay-gi-na-tah
WAR CHIEF = COMMANDING OFFICER

Jay-sho
BUZZARD = BOMBER PLANE

Lo-tso
WHALE = BATTLESHIP

Tacheene
RED SOIL = BATTALION

Tas-chizzie
SWALLOW = TORPEDO PLANE

Toh-ta
BETWEEN WATERS = GREAT BRITAIN

Modern military uniform camouflage began after the French, wearing bright red pantaloons, were defeated by the Germans in a 1915 World War I battle.

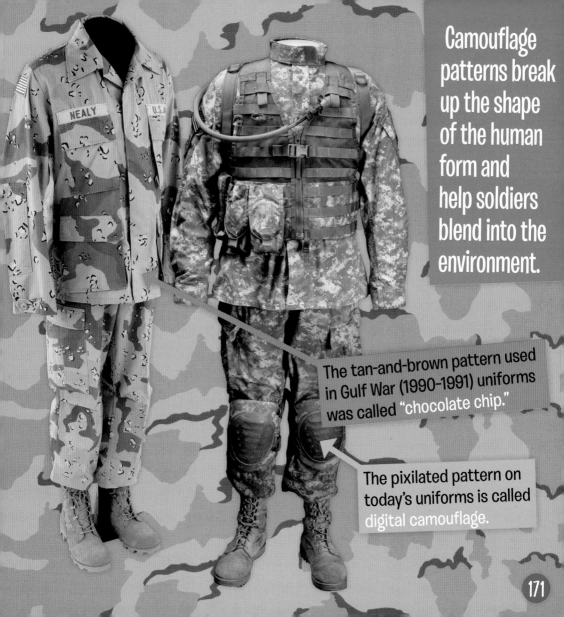

Camouflage patterns break up the shape of the human form and help soldiers blend into the environment.

The tan-and-brown pattern used in Gulf War (1990–1991) uniforms was called "chocolate chip."

The pixilated pattern on today's uniforms is called digital camouflage.

NEALY

U.S.A

Camouflage hid military equipment soldiers, and precious works of art during both world wars.

173

THE PATTERN ON THIS
WORLD WAR I PLANE IS CALLED
LOZENGE CAMOUFLAGE.

Smoky gray camouflage was used for this World War II German night flyer.

290202

During World War II, the US Navy painted the Grumman F4F Wildcat blue-gray so it blended in with the sea and sky.

The black paint on this SR-71 Blackbird absorbs radar signals and camouflages the aircraft against the dark sky at high altitudes.

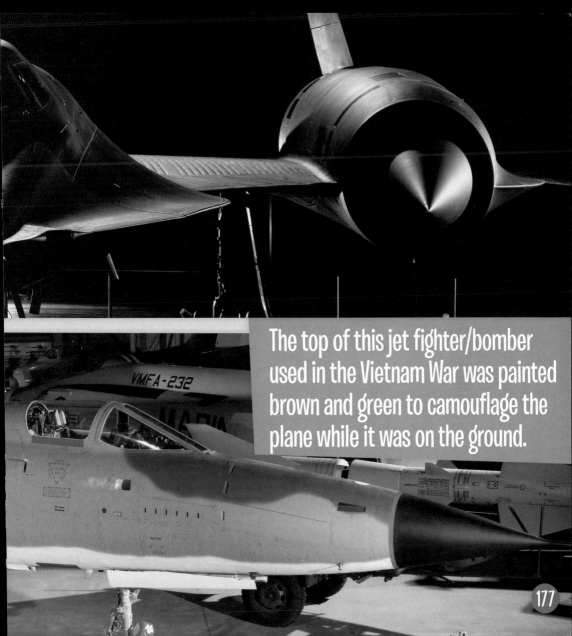

The top of this jet fighter/bomber used in the Vietnam War was painted brown and green to camouflage the plane while it was on the ground.

There are about 2,000 satellites orbiting Earth right now.

Some satellites are spies in the sky, taking photos of Earth below.

Want to know if a spy satellite has you in its sights? There's an app for that!

178

The US military spy satellite program, Project Corona, produced 800,000 images of the Soviet Union and other countries between 1960 and 1972.

Corona satellite re-entry capsule

UNMANNED AERIAL VEHICLES (UAVS) LIKE THIS PIONEER RQ-2A AND RQ-7A SHADOW 200 ARE USED FOR AERIAL SURVEILLANCE BY THE MILITARY.

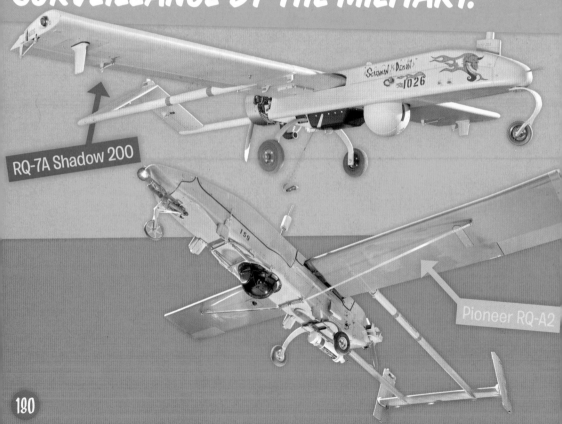

RQ-7A Shadow 200

Pioneer RQ-A2

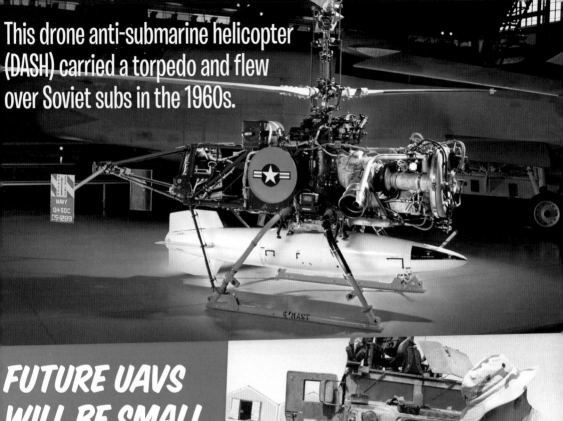

This drone anti-submarine helicopter (DASH) carried a torpedo and flew over Soviet subs in the 1960s.

FUTURE UAVS WILL BE SMALL ENOUGH TO FIT IN THE PALM OF YOUR HAND.

SNEAKY PLANTS and ANIMALS

THE BURROWING OWL PUTS MAMMAL DUNG AROUND ITS UNDERGROUND NEST. DUNG BEETLES COME TO CHECK IT OUT, AND THE OWL EATS THEM. PRETTY SNEAKY!

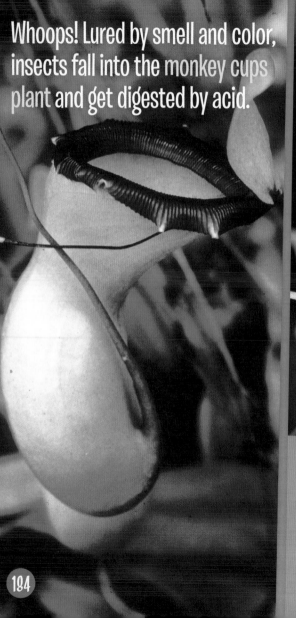

Whoops! Lured by smell and color, insects fall into the monkey cups plant and get digested by acid.

Gotcha! When a water flea hits a trigger hair of a bladderwort, it gets sucked up into a bladder-like trap and a door closes, preventing escape.

Snap! The sensitive leaves of a Venus flytrap snap shut like jaws when insects walk across them.

Sneaky Poison: Poison ivy looks like a regular plant, but if you accidentally touch it, you'll get a terrible rash!

Dogs don't get rashes from poison ivy.

The oily substance in **poison ivy** that gives you a rash is also found in mango skins and in cashews before they are roasted.

Deer can eat poison ivy leaves.

The trapdoor spider covers its burrow with a hinged trapdoor. When insects pass by . . . surprise!

A scorpion fish hides in crevices in coral reefs, then swims out to gobble down prey.

A GOLDEN POISON DART FROG HAS ENOUGH VENOM TO KILL 10 ADULT HUMANS.

A **crocodile** lurks in a watering hole—and lunges out and grabs thirsty animals in its jaws.

A great white shark stalks prey from below—then suddenly shoots upward to attack.

A seahorse clings to plants or coral by its tail and sucks up small prey swimming by.

Leaf insects don't start to look like leaves until they start eating leaves.

JUST A TASTELESS TWIG, NO SNEAKY STICK INSECT HERE, NO WAY. (. . . WAY!)

SOME CATERPILLARS DISGUISE THEMSELVES TO LOOK LIKE BIRD POOP SO THAT BIRDS WON'T EAT THEM.

Chameleons change color for camouflage

and to express emotions such as fear.

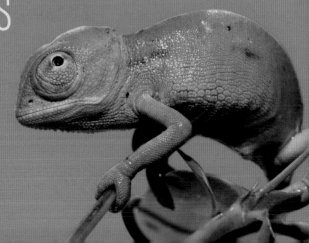

A cuttlefish can change color and shape to disguise itself.

Tiny muscles in the cuttlefish's pigment sacs pull the little color balls in and out.

The okapi's stripes help it hide in dense vegetation so that leopards don't spot it.

Leaf? Bark?

NO WAY!

It's a leaf-tailed gecko, hiding from predators.

Check out these eastern screech owls doing their tree impersonations.

The devil horns of the satanic leaf-tailed gecko break up the silhouette of its body to make it harder to find.

Black herons form a canopy with their wings to make fish think it's nighttime—so they slow down and are easier to catch!

OPOSSUMS PLAY DEAD SO THEY DON'T BECOME DINNER.

A fish called "the sleeper" also plays dead—
and then pops up to gobble down prey.

Cuckoo bees
sneak into
other bees'
hives to lay
their eggs.

When their own food is scarce, squirrels sneak into human homes to snack.

The city-dwelling rhesus macaque will swipe groceries right from a shopper's bag.

Sperm whales hang out in fishing spots to snatch the catch on fishermen's lines.

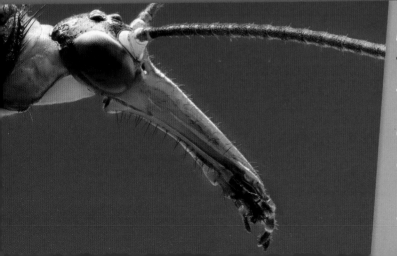

A male **scorpion fly** pretends to be female, accepts a food gift from another male, then re-gifts it to a real female fly.

201

Aquarium-dwelling octopuses have been known to sneak out of their tanks at night to steal crabs from other tanks.

A seagull will steal a fish right from a pelican's bill!

The white coat of the **arctic fox** helps it blend into snow so it can steal eggs from birds' nests.

A large hyena clan can chase away a lion and steal its catch.

INDEX

PHOTO CREDITS